NOT How to Photograph a Hummingbird

by Elaine A. Powers

Illustrated by Anderson Atlas

How (Not) to Photograph a Hummingbird
by Elaine A. Powers

Copyright 2017 by Elaine A. Powers
All rights reserved.

ISBN-13: 978-1979729727
ISBN-10: 1979729727

Published by Lyric Power Publishing LLC, Tucson AZ 2017

No part of this publication may be reproduced or retransmitted in any form or by any means, including, but not limited to, electronic, mechanical, photocopying, recording, or any information storage or retrieval system, without prior written permission of the publisher or copyright holder. Unauthorized copying may subject violators to criminal penalties as well as liability for substantial monetary damages, costs, and attorney's fees.

All information provided is believed and intended to be reliable, but accuracy cannot be guaranteed by the author or the publisher.

How *NOT* to Photograph a Hummingbird

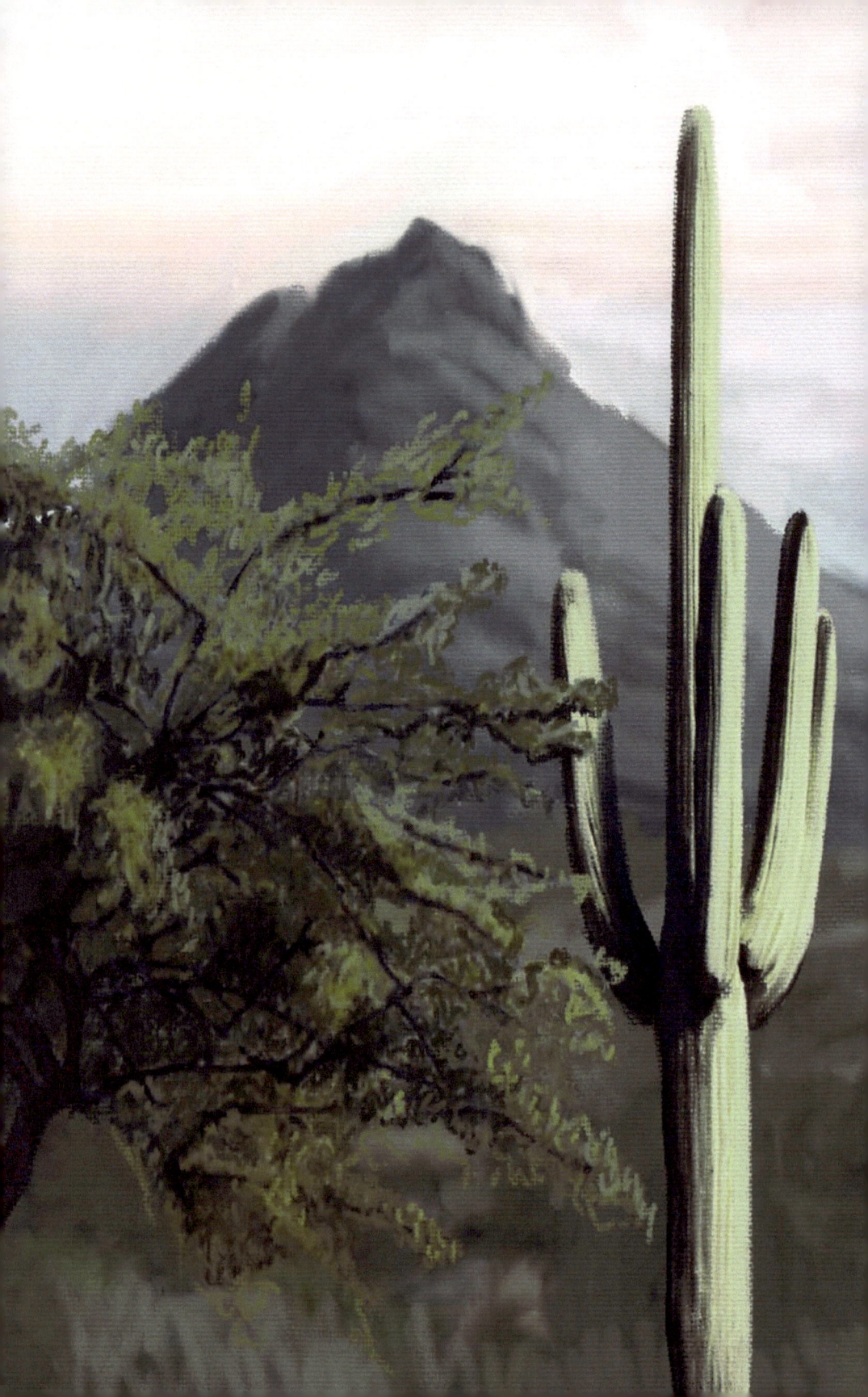

"Welcome to Tucson," said Anna, opening the door of her home.

"Hey, Anna. It's great to see you. Thanks for putting me up overnight. I can't believe they cancelled my flight. 'Course I can't believe they routed me through Tucson in the first place. Oh well, this will give us a chance to catch up and you can show me that garden of yours that you're always talking about. I confess, I can't imagine it's too much of a garden. Leastways compared to out East, judging by the desolate desert I passed coming from the airport. But I'll keep an open mind. Nice adobe house, by the way. Guess you don't have much use for vinyl siding out here, do you?"

I entered Anna's rather spacious house. "Love the tile work on the floor. Does it get slippery in the rain? Oh wait, that's right, this is a desert. No rain. Dry heat and all."

"Welcome. Come on in. I'm so glad you're able to visit, even if it is unintentional. Leave your bag here and come out onto the patio. Would you like something to drink?" Anna asked.

"No, the driver made me drink a bottle of water," I replied. "Lectured me on staying hydrated. Drinking water is apparently a big pastime here." I walked through the cool darkness of the house interior back out into the bright Arizona sunshine.

"Wow," I said, squinting while my eyes adjusted to the searing sunlight. The yard was filled with all sorts of plants. I recognized the large saguaro cactus. Hey, I've seen my share of Westerns. Between the tall cactus with arms in the 'reach for the sky, pardner' pose were bright orange trumpet flower bushes and fruit trees. These alternated with bushes covered in purple flowers and some with red spikey flowers.

My attention was drawn to a tree with thin branches and green bark. I reached up to take a closer look at the lovely yellow flowers and stabbed my finger on a huge thorn. "What's this deadly tree?"

"It's a palo verde," replied Anna. "That's green stick in Spanish."

"Yeah, what's with all the Spanish here? It's like everywhere in this town."

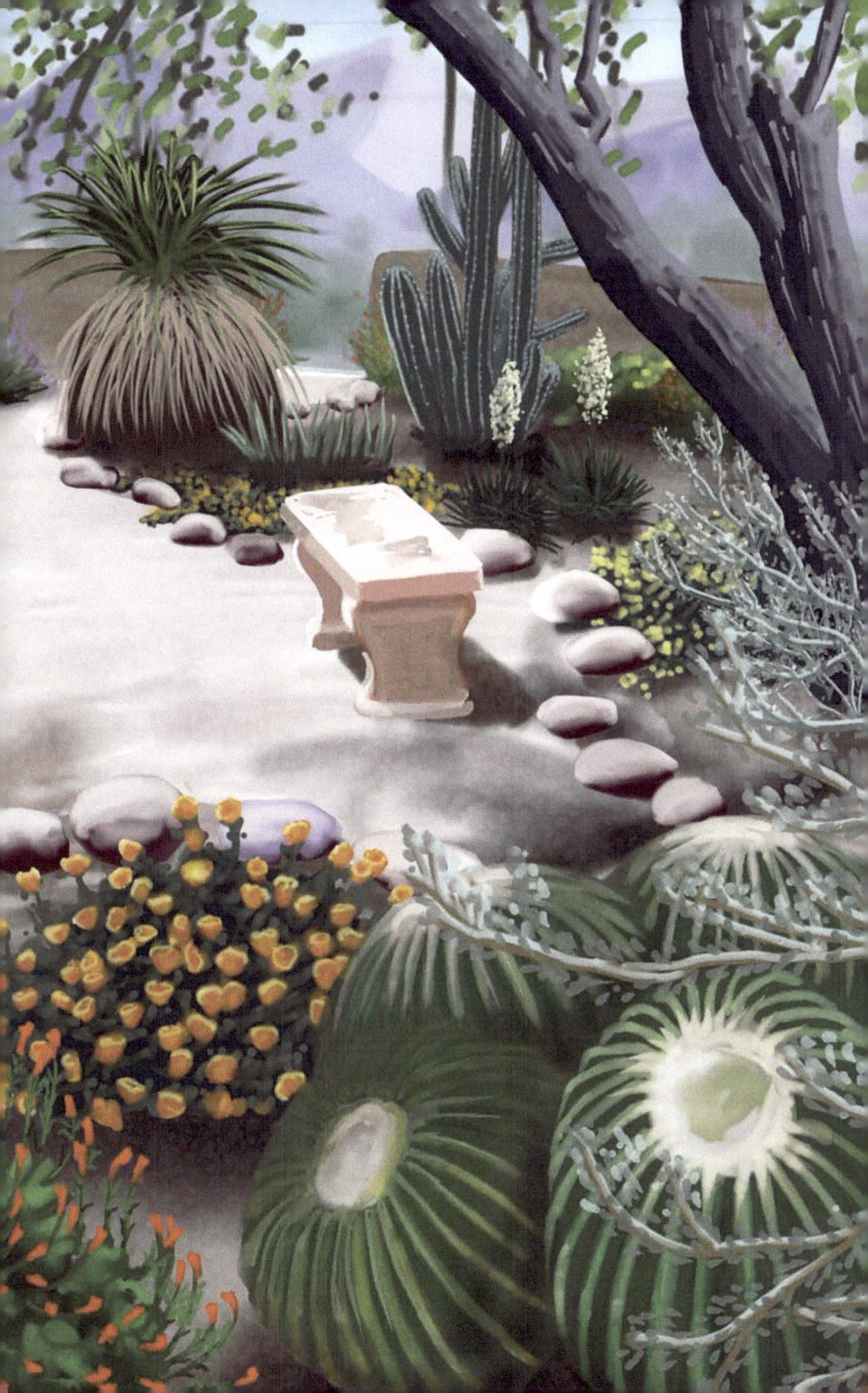

"Arizona was once part of Mexico. You remember the Gadsen Purchase? Fortunately, much of the culture was preserved. It gives Tucson diversity," she replied.

"Yeah, speaking of diversity, why all the bird feeders around your garden?"

"I like birds," Anna replied. "I have nectar feeders for the hummingbirds, thistle seed, or more accurately Nyjer seed, for the goldfinches, sunflower seeds for the larger finches, northern and desert cardinals, and seed blocks for the quail and doves. Of course, the doves and quail also attract the birds of prey. All birds are welcome."

"Hey, I know my hummers, Anna. I put out fuchsia for them on my deck back east." A hummingbird zipped into front of me.

"What a magnificent male Anna's hummingbird. Were you named after it? Great bird. We don't get those at home," I said to my friend.

"I need a photo." I whipped up my cell phone, conveniently held in my hand, aimed it toward the hummingbird that hovered in front of me, flashing his brilliant red-purple gorget, that's what the neck feathers are called. It's a handy term to know when playing word games.

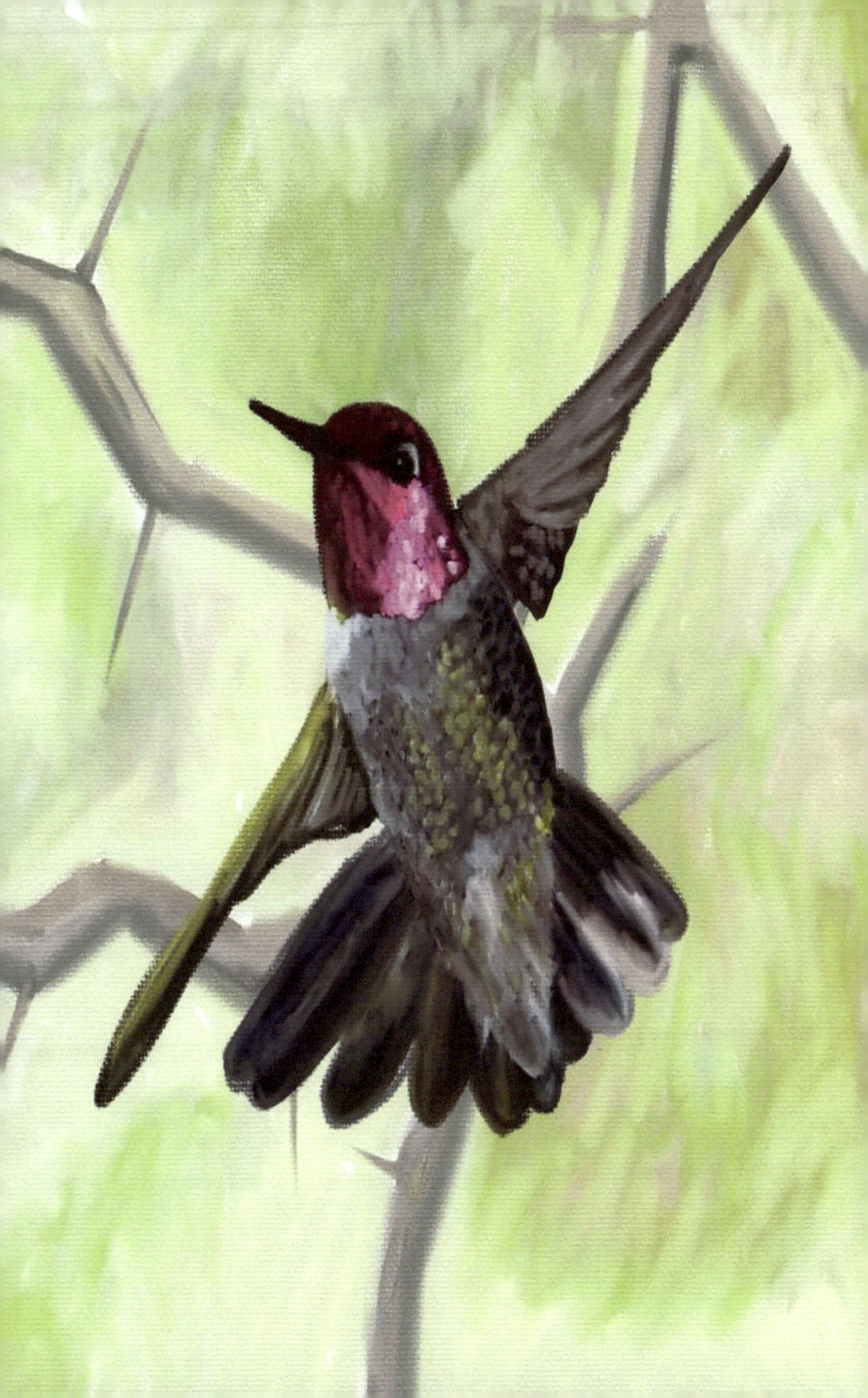

I aimed. The bird zipped to the left. I followed, tripping over a big chunk of decorative malachite-azurite rock.

"Be careful", Anna said, bending over to upright the rock. I didn't know if she was worried about me or the rock. It was a lovely mix of green and blue. It's supposed to have positive energy, but I wasn't feeling it just then. I snapped a quick picture of the minerals glinting in the sunlight, stood up and looked for my original subject.

He zipped back in front of me, hovering, his wings thrumming in the air. I snapped a quick photo of… nothing.

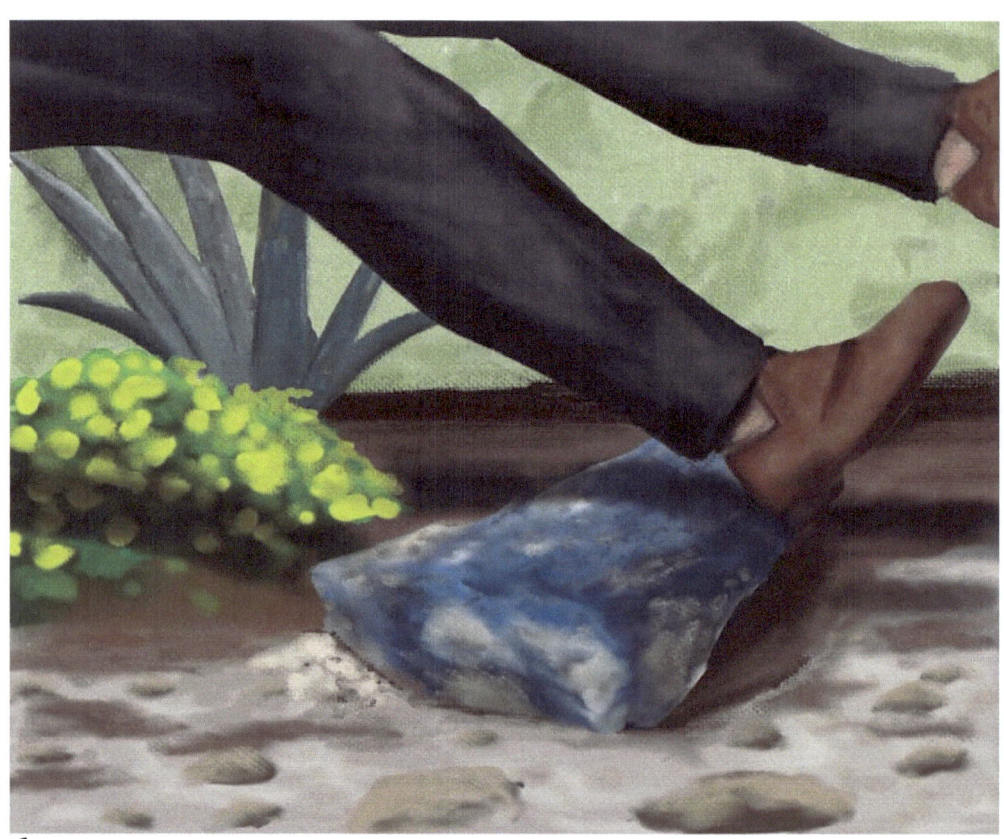

The hummingbird had flitted to the other side of a bush. Around it I went in pursuit. The ground erupted into scurrying bird bodies and the air was filled with a sound like "wa-wop," coming from the panicked Gambel's quail. I stopped in place until the fleeing subsided. The hummingbird zipped back in front of me.

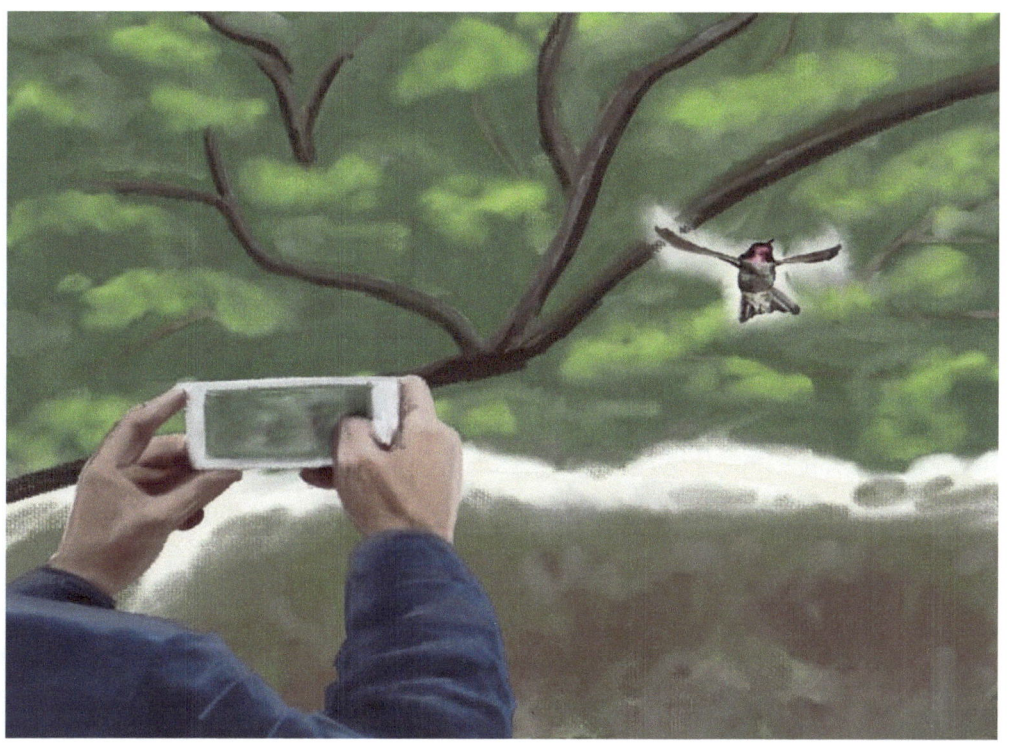

Okay, he was playing with me. Sure, he'd flit over to the nectar-filled bird feeder for a quick sip, but then he'd be back in front of me. Did he see me as a challenger for his territory? Was I a threat to his male ego? Or did he realize I was trying to take a photograph and knew that a minimum number of seconds were required for the camera to focus. How did he know? Do the hummingbirds get together and discuss these things? I've heard them chik-chik-chiking in the morning. Maybe that's what they talk about.

Once again, the hummingbird zipped away, this time to the right. I went after him. This was no longer about a photograph; I would not be outwitted by a mere bird. On my third step, my foot sank into the ground. A ground squirrel tunnel collapsed into my shoe. I lost my balance and reached for a branch to steady myself so I wouldn't fall. My hand closed around the branch as I realized it was a mesquite tree.

I use a lot of mesquite in my barbequing, but my wood chips don't have thorns. These mesquite thorns sank deep into the flesh of my hand. Fortunately, the thorns remained attached to the tree and pulled out when I withdrew my hand, now featuring a rivulet of crimson blood. My blood. It added additional color to the scene. Anna handed me a tissue, which I wound around my hand.

"Want to wash out your wound?" Anna asked.

"No, I'm tough, a little scratch like this won't stop me," I replied and continued my pursuit. There, poised at eye level on a branch, sat the hummingbird. I stepped cautiously closer, crunching the dry leaves beneath my feet. I hoped the crunching wouldn't scare the bird. Crunch, rattle.

A rapid rattle arose from near my feet. Was that a cicada? I'd like to get a close-up photo of a cicada. Impressive insects. So prehistoric looking. But I'd wait until I'd gotten a shot of the hummingbird, of course. The rapid rattling got louder as I realized a cicada wouldn't be at my feet. I stopped. I looked down, knowing with increasing fear that the sound wasn't a cicada but another common resident of the Sonoran Desert.

There, coiled with his head rising, was a Western Diamondback rattlesnake. A small one, fortunately, with a gorgeous pattern.

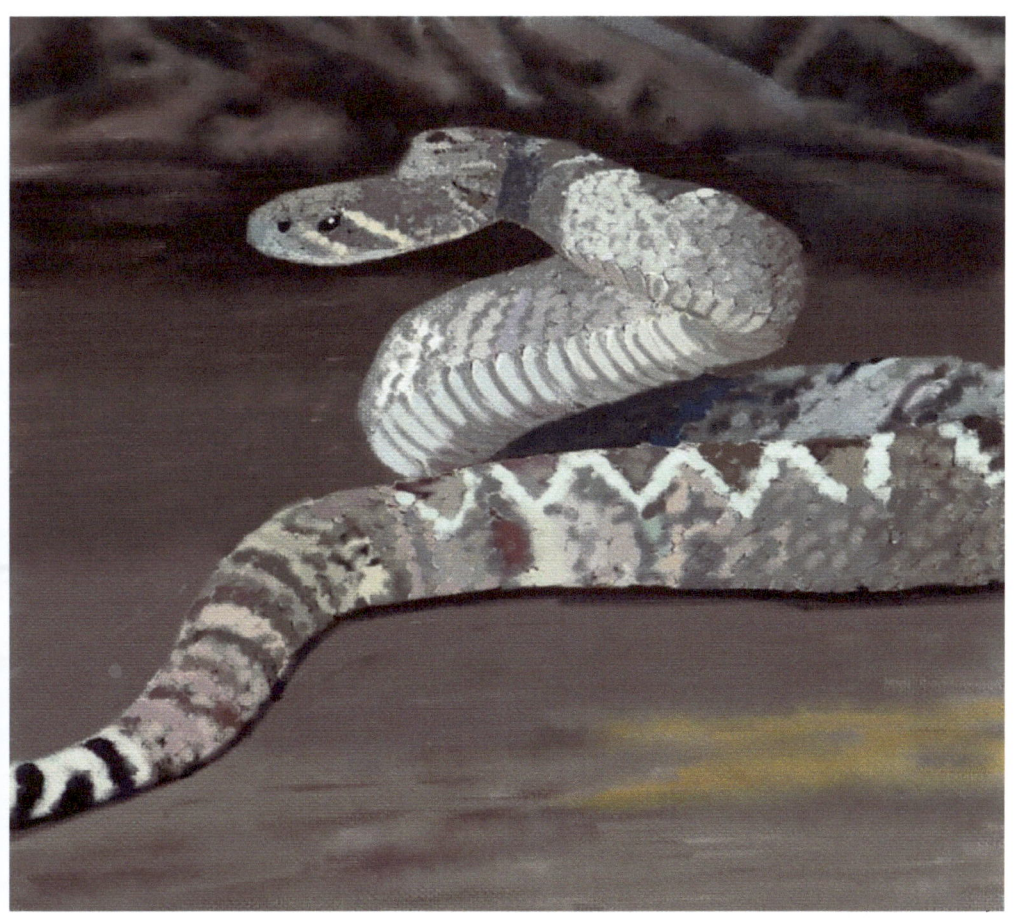

I took a few quick photographs, happily the snake stayed in one place, and stepped backward to give the snake some space.

You know, in those safety talks about hiking in the desert, they mention looking behind you before stepping backwards. It's good advice in gardens, too. I stepped back directly into a cholla, a Teddy Bear cholla. Teddy bear cholla look so soft and fuzzy. But they're not.

I felt the spines sinking into the back of my calf. I didn't look. I didn't want to look. I'd have a long-term reminder of this visit. Maybe a permanent one. I clenched my teeth, so Anna wouldn't hear the scream emanating from my throat. I took a moment while the wave of pain subsided.

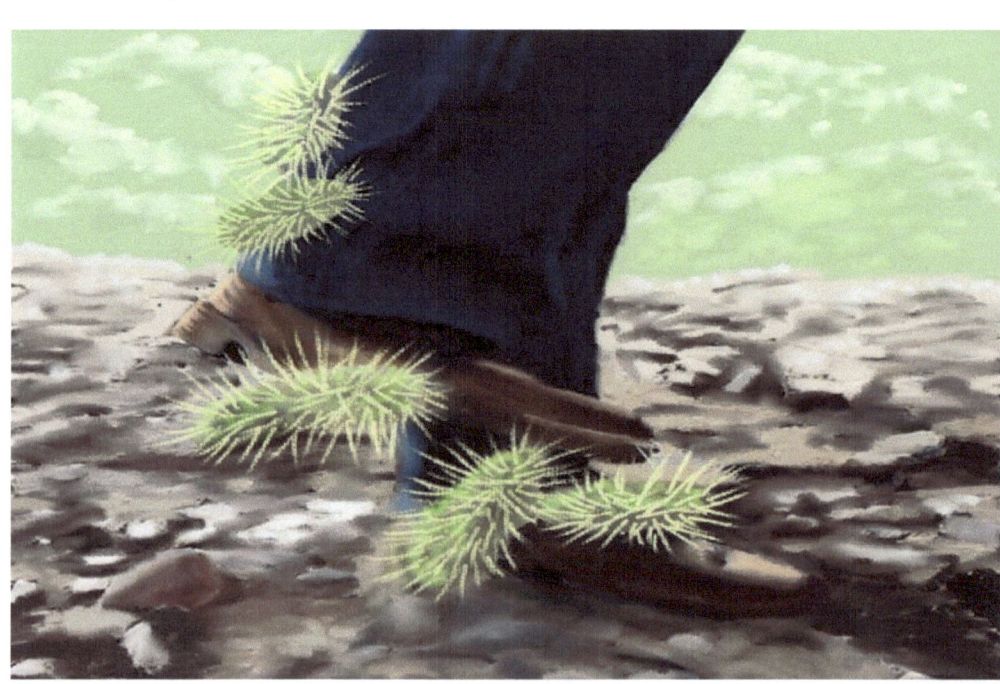

I clenched my cell phone tightly in my tissue-wrapped hand. That's it. No more Mister Nice Guy. I was going to photograph that hummingbird. I was not going to lose this battle. It was now a matter of honor.

Where was my opponent? There! He was perfectly perched on an upper branch. The snake had moved off, a wise choice given my current mood. I stepped closer cautiously aiming the camera lens.

Focusing, focusing. Another step. Enlarging. I rested my foot upon a gray rock, leaned forward, my finger descending toward the camera button. The rock hissed and heaved. I lurched backward. The rock raised itself up, a head emerged, and two dark eyes with white rims glared at me. A Sonoran Desert Tortoise. I had stepped on a Sonoroan Desert Tortoise!

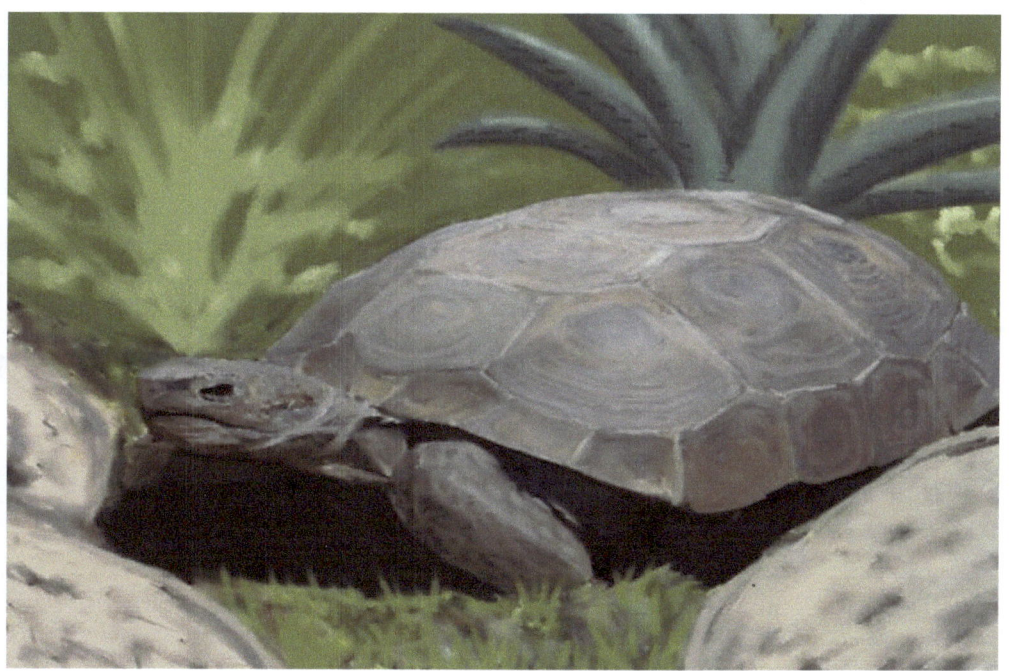

"Don't step on the tortoise," Anna shouted.

"I'm sorry," I said to the back of the tortoise as he stomped off.

My friend chased after the reptile and checked to be sure I hadn't injured him.

Chastened, I returned more humbly to the hummingbird. He zipped back and forth through the branches, stopping now and then for a quick sip, then off and about. He was taunting me. Even the Gila Woodpecker high in the palo verde tree was laughing at me.

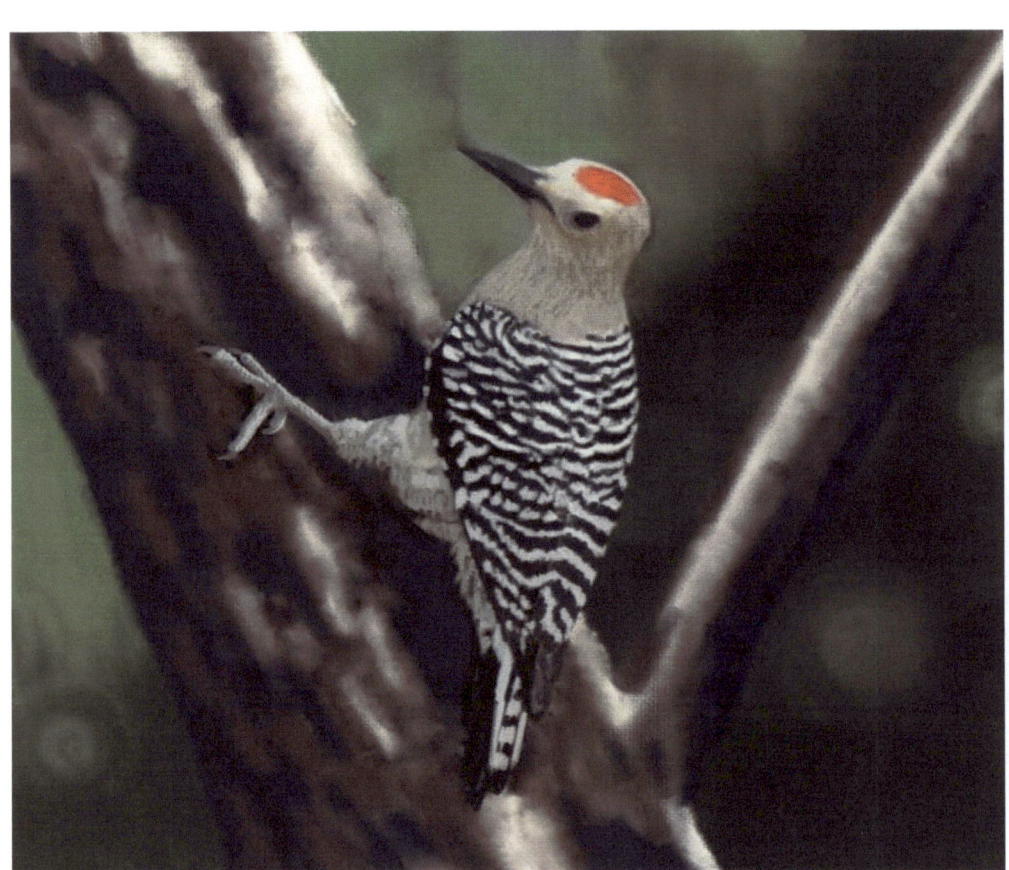

"Come on," I pleaded. "One photo. That's all I want, one photo of your magnificent iridescent feathers." Those words seemed to catch the bird's attention. He hovered above me, as if contemplating. Maybe vanity existed in hummingbirds. I pointed the camera toward the bird. He hovered. I pressed the button to center. Now! I pushed the button. The hummingbird flew directly at my face! I leaned back and ducked. The cell phone leapt from my hand, somersaulted in the air and landed in the depression made by the departed tortoise.

Whew, at least it didn't fall near the hose. I wouldn't want it to get wet.

Anna's red hose had a lovely pattern. I'd never seen one that color. My hoses at home were dark green. I wondered what brand it was. Maybe it was specially designed for the hot summer sun. I reached to pick up my phone and the hose at the same time. The hose rose to meet my hand. A head swung around to greet me, face to face.

"Oh good," said Anna. "Quick, take a picture of the coachwhip snake, please. I've been trying to get one for months."

I like my friend, really I do. But she needed to work on her priorities.

I was face-to-face with a large red snake who obviously was not intimidated by my superior size, but who was certainly intimidating me, and her concern was a photograph? I could be bitten. I could be bitten on the face!

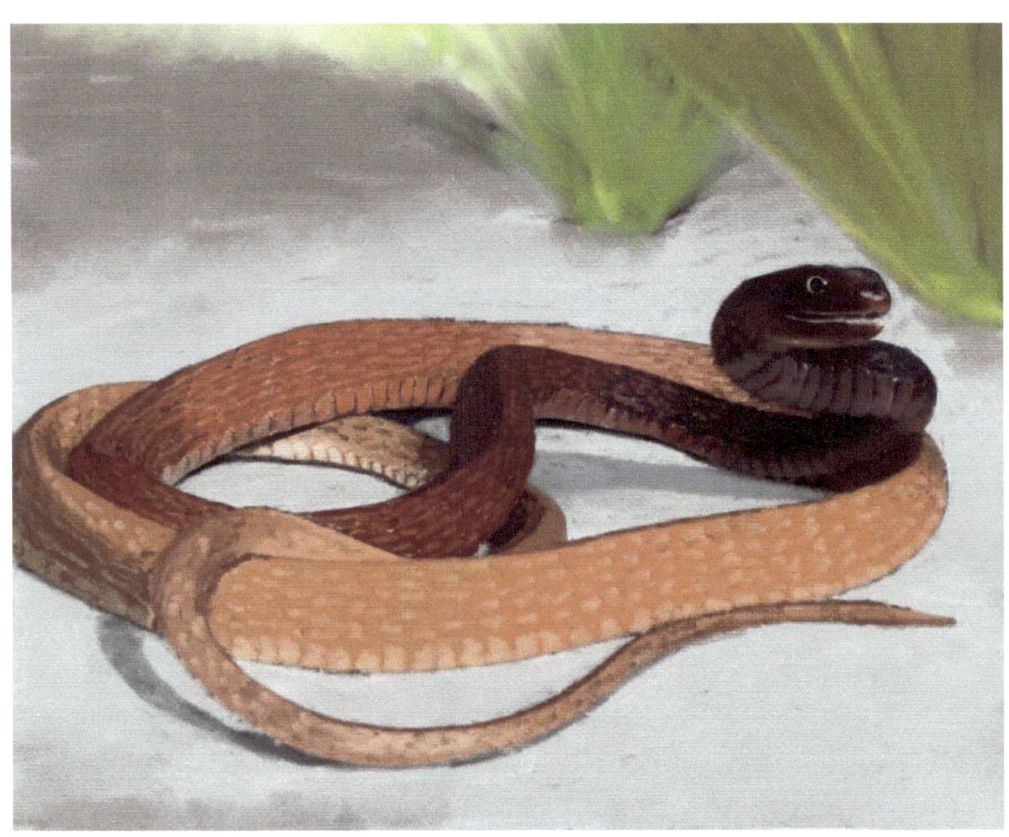

But I did have the camera in my hand and I was close enough for a great shot, so I snapped several photos as the snake obligingly held his position, reminiscent of a cobra. He was not going to back down, so I backed up once again, but this time looking behind me. A desert spiny lizard shot up from beneath the leaves of a shrub, startling me, and I fell.

The snake's face was now higher than mine. I thought about rolling away but the pain in my leg reminded me of the plant hazards. The hummingbird zipped down to me. I think he was checking to be sure I was all right.

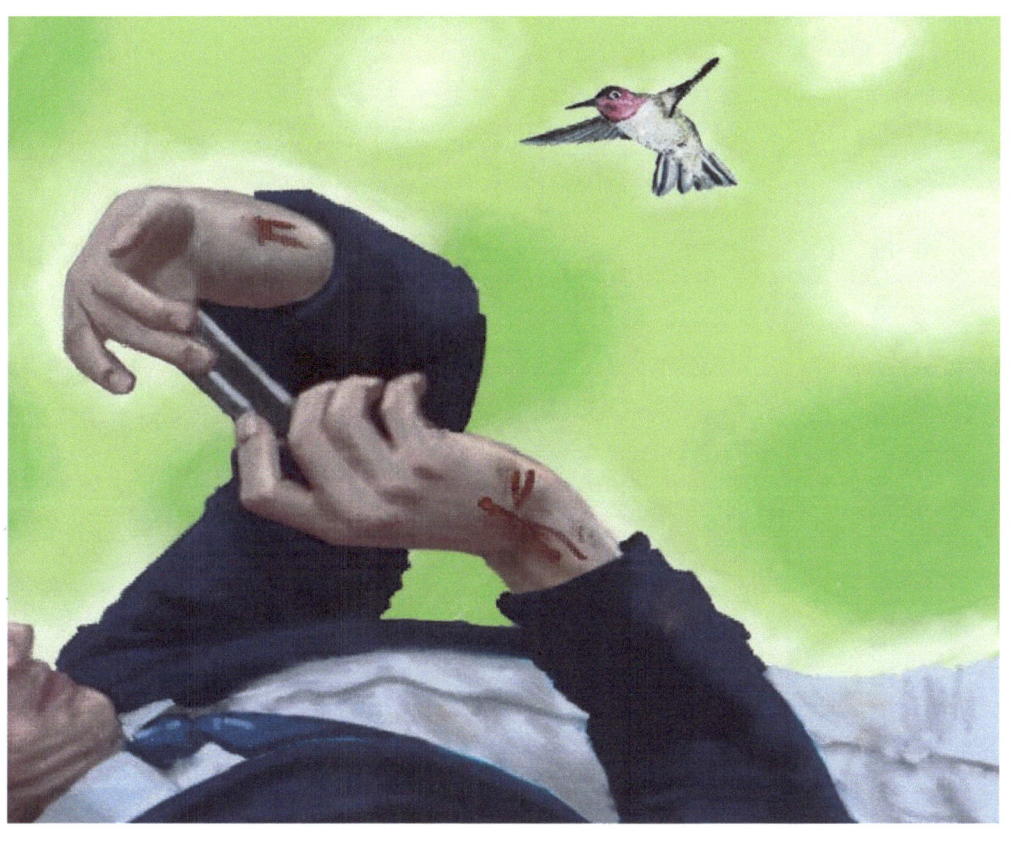

As I got to my knees, the snake felt victorious and slithered away. I admired the undulation as he headed off.

Once again upright, I debated the necessity of a photograph. The hummingbird zipped in front of me to assure me that, yes, a photo was required. He perched on a branch directly in front of me. The surrounding vegetation framed him perfectly. I leaned in, composing what was going to be an award winning photo, and flash! Yellow filled my view screen. The shock of a robin-sized yellow bird swooping at me caused me to stumble backward. I looked up. Both the hummingbird and I watched as a Hooded Oriole landed on the nectar feeder.

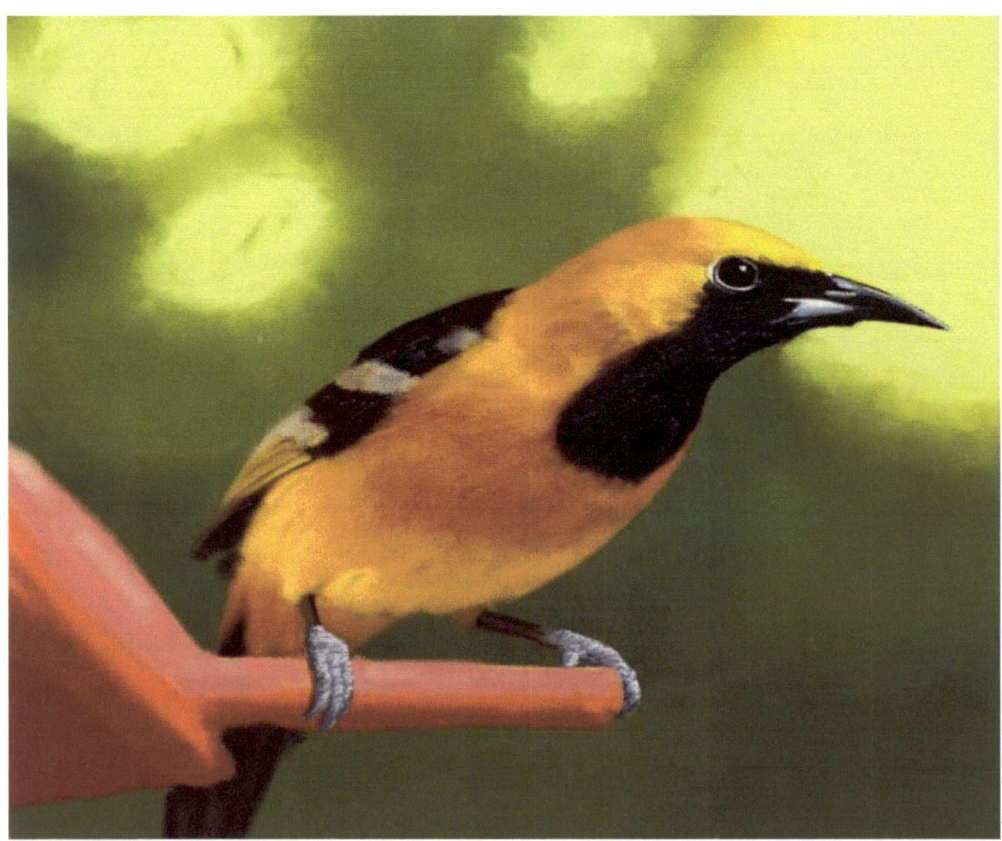

The large bird held on as the feeder swung. "Okay, I'll take your photo," I said to the oriole once I had recovered my composure. I took several photos then returned to my original quarry.

"Okay," I said, holding up my phone with the dirty blood-soaked tissue-covered hand toward the hummingbird once again hovering in front of me.

He landed on a branch and perched motionless. "Perfect," I said as I carefully aimed the camera. "I'm going to get it, I'm finally going to get the shot," I said. Just as I tapped the button, the hummingbird zipped away, then zipped back to land on top of my phone.

The hummingbird looked up at me and chiked. He tilted his head and flashed his gorget. With one last chik, he rose into the air, hovered, flashed and zipped away into the sky.

"Did you get it?" Anna asked.

"No," I replied. I wasn't unhappy about it, though. I had met a very special bird and shared a moment with him. I didn't need a photograph.

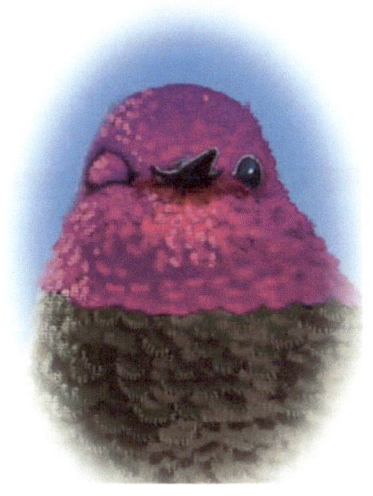

APPENDIX

Anna's Hummingbird (*Calypte anna*) This medium-sized hummingbird is found along the Pacific Coast and into the desert Southwest. It is the 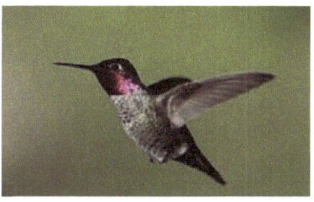 only hummingbird that remains in the West during the winter. Named after Princess Anna de Belle Massena, an Anna's is identified by its iridescent emerald feathers and bright pink gorget, or throat feathers. *(Photo by USFWS Pacific Southwest Region)*

Azurite is a deep blue-colored copper mineral, $Cu_3(CO_3)_2(OH)_2$. This carbonate mineral has been utilized since ancient times; it is mentioned by Pliny the Elder in his 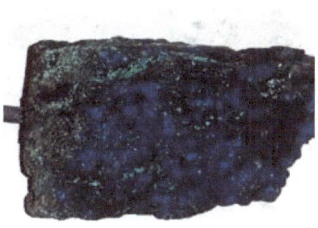 *Natural History*. Azurite crystals are often found with the closely related mineral Malachite. In fact, azurite can undergo chemical changes to become Malachite. In many cultures, azurite is believed to have strong psychic powers, providing energy. *(Photo by the author)*

Coachwhip (*Masticophis flagellum cingulum*) is a slender nonvenomous snake with variable coloring to help in camouflage. In Tucson, coachwhips that are pink to 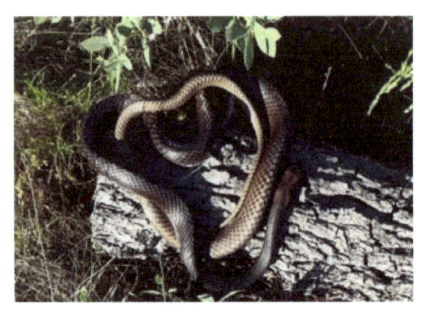 red in color are called red racers. The pattern on the scales give the snake a braided look like an old-time leather coach whip. Their large eyes provide good eyesight. In times of trouble, they prefer to rapidly slither away (considered one of the fastest snakes) but, if cornered, they will rise up, hiss, vibrate the tip of its tail to simulate the sound of a rattlesnake, and strike quickly and repeatedly. The coachwhip is associated with several Western fables. One is that the snake bites onto its own tail to form a hoop, then rolls in pursuit of its prey. Another is that a coachwhip will chase a person, coil around him, and then lash him to death with its tail. The snake checks the person for life by inserting its tail into the person's nose. If the person isn't dead, the snake will continue the lashing. Of course, none of these stories is true. (*Photo by Clinton & Charles Robertson*)

Desert Spiny Lizard (*Sceloporus magister*) is a large, stocky lizard of southwestern Arizona that eats insects, arachnids, small lizards, and some plants. 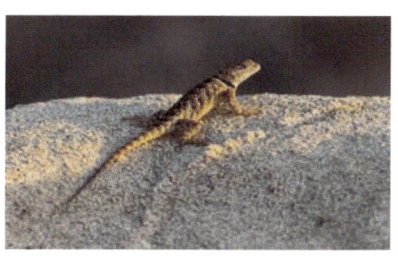 The overlapping gray and brown scales are pointed and keeled. The male's body features a purple stripe near the neck. *(Photo by Joshua Tree National Park)*

Gambel's Quail (*Callipepla gambelii*) These plump, ground-dwelling birds of the desert Southwest are named after William Gambel. The 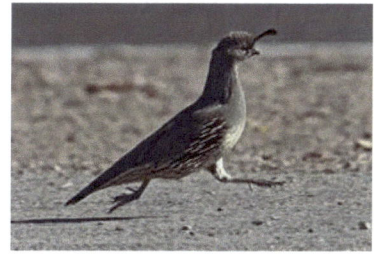 bluish-gray birds are easily identified by the feather plume on their heads. Quail use camouflage to avoid their many predators. The average lifespan is a year and a half. The chicks are precocial, leaving the nest to follow and feed with their parents within hours after hatching. *(Photo by Lip Kee Yap)*

Gila Woodpecker (*Melanerpes uropygialis*) This common woodpecker in southern Arizona is often seen on saguaro cactus. They have a 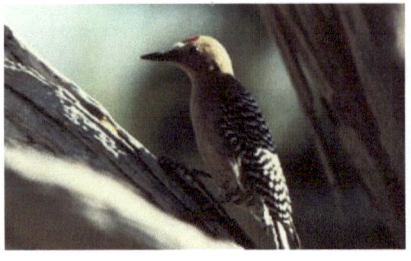 distinctive horizontally barred black-and-white back with a plain brown head. The male's head is adorned with a red crown patch. They excavate nests in Saguaros and mesquite trees, and the abandoned cavities are later used by a variety of other animals. *(Photo Public domain from USFWS.)*

Hooded Oriole (*Icterus cucullatus*) These spectacularly colored orioles have yellow-orange bodies and black faces and wings. The medium-sized birds are known to drink 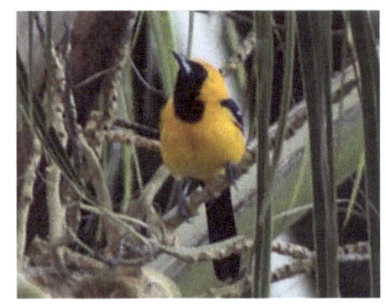 from hummingbird feeders, even when doing so requires acrobatics. Nests are sewn to the underside of overhanging large leaves, such as palm fronds. *(Wikipedia photo by Tony Hisgett)*

Malachite ($Cu_2CO_3(OH)_2$) is the other common copper carbonate mineral found in the Sonoran Desert. This bright green rock is named after the color of the mallow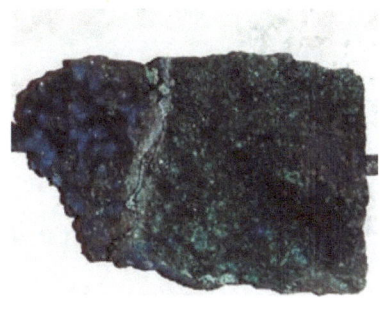
plant. Malachite is often found embedded with blue azurite, and in polished form, the combination is said to resemble Mother Earth. Besides their chemical properties, they are believed to provide a powerful blend of healing energies. *(Photo by the author)*

Mesquite, Velvet (*Prosopis velutina*) This thorny native tree of the Sonoran Desert survives the dry climate by sinking a taproot deep into the earth. The thorns reach one inch in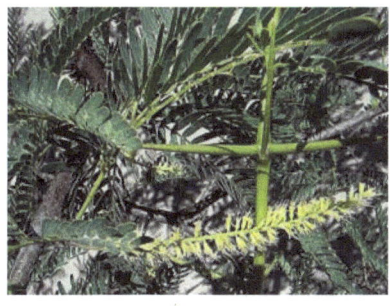
length. The tree is an important part of the ecosystem, providing food and protection for animals and people. Flour is made from the seed pods. The wood is popular for grilling and seasoning food, and for carving into utensils. *(Wikipedia photo by Dick Culbert)*

Palo Verde, Foothills (*Parkinsonia microphylla*) Palo verde means *green stick* in Spanish. It is so named due to its green bark, which, unlike the bark of other trees, 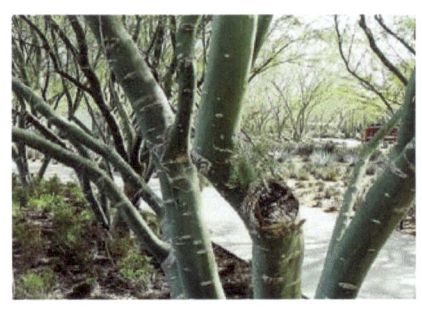 is capable of photosynthesis. The tree is also known for its spines, seed pods, and brilliant yellow flowers. Palo verdes play a vital role in the Sonoran Desert ecology, serving as the primary nurse plant for young saguaro cacti. The genus name *Parkinsonia* honors the English botanist John Parkinson. *(Wikipedia photo by "inkknife_2000")*

Round-tailed Ground Squirrel (*Spermophilus tereticaudus*) Despite looking and acting like small prairie dogs, ground squirrels are unrelated. Instead of a fluffy tail like their tree- 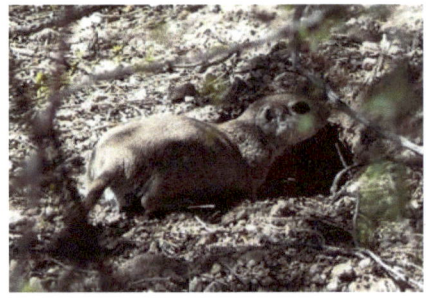 dwelling cousins, ground squirrels have a long round tail. They are omnivores and live in extensive burrows, although they spend a great deal of time on the surface during the day. Their sandy color matches the soil they burrow in. *(Wikipedia photo by "sue in az")*

Saguaro (*Carnegiea gigantean*) These tree-sized, columnar cacti are the symbol of the West and are important part of the Sonoran Desert ecosystem for both animals and humans. The saguaro is the largest cactus in 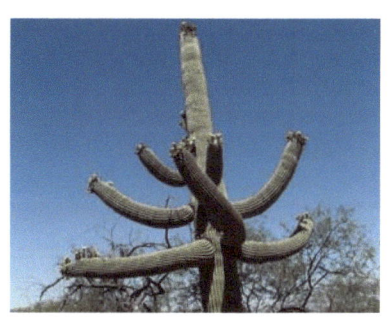 the United States and its crown of large white blooms is honored as Arizona's state flower. The saguaro grows very slowly but can live a couple of centuries. They may or may not develop branches or "arms." The roots are very shallow, extending out as far as the saguaro's height, but the cactus is also anchored by one deep tap root. The scientific name honors Andrew Carnegie. *(Photo by the author)*

Sonoran Desert Tortoise (*Gopherus morafkai*) This tortoise has adapted to the extreme environment of the Sonoran Desert. It has powerful limbs covered with thick 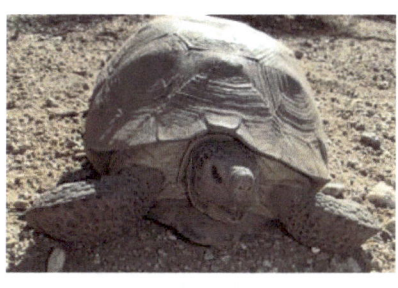 scaly skin for digging underground burrows where it spends much of its time. It eats a wide variety of plants including many that are indigestible to other animals. It feeds most actively during the monsoon season, and is dormant much of the rest of the year. The tortoise stores water in its bladder, going up to a year without drinking. As a defense mechanism, the tortoise will empty its bladder to discourage a predator, like other reptiles. Unfortunately, this can deplete its water supply and result in death during a drought. For this reason, it is important to never pick up or interfere with a desert tortoise. The gravest danger to the desert tortoises is human-caused mortality. The scientific name honors Joseph Morafka for his work with tortoises. *(Photo by author)*

Teddy Bear Cholla (*Cylindropuntia bigelovii*). From a distance, this cactus looks soft and fuzzy, but it is actually covered in a dense mass of spines. The spines, 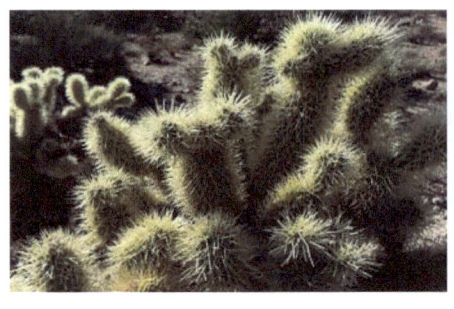 which are a form of leaf, are about an inch long, ending in a hook or barb. These spines so easily detach and embed in the flesh of any animal that touches it, that it is also called the Jumping Cholla, as if it can actually attack passing animals. *(Photo by author)*

Western Diamondback Rattlesnake (*Crotalus atrox*) This snake is known for its distinctive rattle when threatened. The keratin rattle mechanism at the tip of the tail 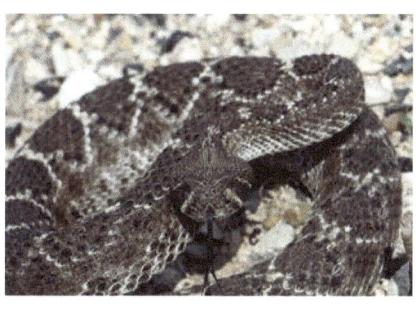 twitches up to 50 times per second. The dark diamond-shaped pattern on its back identifies this common Tucson rattler. Rattlesnakes belong to a group of venomous snakes called pit vipers, and are found in a wide range of habitats. The pits, located between the nostrils and the eyes, are used in sensing the heat of other animals, and are sensitive enough to detect a body only a fraction of a degree warmer than the ambient air. Rattlers usually hunt at night, preferring small nocturnal mammals. Rattlesnakes are important in controlling the populations of disease-carrying rodents. *(Photo by Clinton & Charles Robertson)*

ACKNOWLEDGMENTS

This story was inspired by a young man who chased a hummingbird around the Tucson Botanical Gardens. I don't know if he ever got his photograph but I thank him for the inspiration for this story. I am always thankful for my critique group of Pamela Bickell, Kate J. Steele and Bradley Peterson. I am forever grateful to my editor, Nora Miller, who creates books out of my bits and pieces. Most of all, I am grateful to the flora and fauna of the Sonoran Desert, which bring endless joy to my life.

PHOTO CREDITS

Pacific Southwest Region (https://commons.wikimedia.org/wiki/File:Anna's_hummingbird.jpg), „Anna's hummingbird", https://creativecommons.org/licenses/by/2.0/legalcode

Clinton & Charles Robertson from RAF Lakenheath, UK & San Marcos, TX, USA & UK (https://commons.wikimedia.org/wiki/File:Coachwhip_@_Sawdust_Ranch_(11721609).jpg), „Coachwhip @ Sawdust Ranch (11721609)", https://creativecommons.org/licenses/by-sa/2.0/legalcode

Joshua Tree National Park (https://commons.wikimedia.org/wiki/File:Desert_Spiny_Lizard_(Sceloporus_magister)_(20526596989).jpg), „Desert Spiny Lizard (Sceloporus magister) (20526596989)", https://creativecommons.org/licenses/by/2.0/legalcode

Don Faulkner (https://commons.wikimedia.org/wiki/File:Gambel's_Quail_(17957416199).jpg), „Gambel's Quail (17957416199)", https://creativecommons.org/licenses/by-sa/2.0/legalcode

Tony Hisgett from Birmingham, UK (https://commons.wikimedia.org/wiki/File:Male_Hooded_Oriole_(4355042024).jpg), „Male Hooded Oriole (4355042024)", https://creativecommons.org/licenses/by/2.0/legalcode

Dick Culbert from Gibsons, B.C., Canada (https://commons.wikimedia.org/wiki/File:Prosopis_juliflora,_known_as_the_Velvet_Mesquite_(10078437503).jpg), „Prosopis juliflora, known as the Velvet Mesquite (10078437503)", https://creativecommons.org/licenses/by/2.0/legalcode

inkknife_2000 (7.5 million views +) (https://commons.wikimedia.org/wiki/File:Palo_Verde_Trees_2-22-14a_(12935881964).jpg), „Palo Verde Trees 2-22-14a (12935881964)", cropped by Nora Miller, https://creativecommons.org/licenses/by-sa/2.0/legalcode

Sue in az (https://commons.wikimedia.org/wiki/File:Round_tailed_ground_squirrel.jpg), „Round tailed ground squirrel", https://creativecommons.org/licenses/by-sa/3.0/legalcode

Clinton & Charles Robertson from Del Rio, Texas & College Station, TX, USA (https://commons.wikimedia.org/wiki/File:Western_Diamond-back_Rattlesnake.jpg), „Western Diamondback Rattlesnake", https://creativecommons.org/licenses/by/2.0/legalcode

www.ingramcontent.com/pod-product-compliance
Lightning Source LLC
Chambersburg PA
CBHW041944240526
45473CB00033B/512